TAKE ME TO YOUR SPONSOR

Best Jokes & Cartoons
from AA Grapevine

AA Grapevine, Inc. • New York, NY • www.aagrapevine.org

Books Published by AA Grapevine, Inc.

The Language of the Heart (& eBook)

The Best of the Grapevine Volume I (eBook only)

The Best of Bill (& eBook)

Thank You for Sharing

Spiritual Awakenings (& eBook)

I Am Responsible: The Hand of AA

The Home Group: Heartbeat of AA (& eBook)

Emotional Sobriety — The Next Frontier (& eBook)

Spiritual Awakenings II (& eBook)

In Our Own Words: Stories of Young AAs in Recovery (& eBook)

Beginners' Book (& eBook)

Voices of Long-Term Sobriety (& eBook)

A Rabbit Walks Into A Bar

Step by Step — Real AAs, Real Recovery (& eBook)

Emotional Sobriety II — The Next Frontier (& eBook)

Young & Sober (& eBook)

Into Action (& eBook)

Happy, Joyous & Free (& eBook)

One on One (& eBook)

No Matter What (& eBook)

Grapevine Daily Quote Book (& eBook)

Sober & Out (& eBook)

Forming True Partnerships (& eBook)

Our Twelve Traditions (& eBook)

Making Amends (& eBook)

Voices of Women in AA (& eBook)

AA in the Military (& eBook)

One Big Tent (& eBook)

IN SPANISH

El lenguaje del corazón

Lo mejor de Bill (& eBook)

El grupo base: Corazón de AA Lo mejor de La Viña

Felices, alegres y libres (& eBook)

Un día a la vez (& eBook)

Frente A Frente (& eBook)

IN FRENCH

Le langage du coeur

Les meilleurs articles de Bill

Le Groupe d'attache: Le battement du coeur des AA

En tête à tête (& eBook)

Heureux, joyeux et libres (& eBook)

AA PREAMBLE

Alcoholics Anonymous is a fellowship of men and women who share their experience, strength and hope with each other that they may solve their common problem and help others to recover from alcoholism.

The only requirement for membership is a desire to stop drinking. There are no dues or fees for AA membership; we are self-supporting through our own contributions. AA is not allied with any sect, denomination, politics, organization or institution; does not wish to engage in any controversy, neither endorses nor opposes any causes.

Our primary purpose is to stay sober and help other alcoholics to achieve sobriety.

Contents

Meetings 1

Sponsorship 27

Dating & Marriage 51

Friends, Family, Coworkers 79

Character Defects 103

Gotta Love AA 131

HAVE A LAUGH WITH US

Sobriety can be tough sometimes, which is why recovering alcoholics can always use a good laugh. In AA, we learn to not take ourselves too seriously, to be happy, joyous and free. Luckily, sobriety can be pretty darn amusing.

"Outsiders are sometimes shocked when we burst into merriment over a seemingly tragic experience out of the past," our cofounder, Bill W., writes in *Alcoholics Anonymous*. "But why shouldn't we laugh? We have recovered, and have been given the power to help others."

Two of the most beloved departments of Grapevine are the "At Wit's End" jokes and the cartoons, all contributed and drawn by AA members. This book contains some of the best laughs of the last few years, dealing with meetings, sponsorship, dating and marriage, friends and coworkers, character defects and more. We hope this book brightens your day and gives you some hearty, well-earned laughs.

CHAPTER 1

MEETINGS

"MY FRIEND BARB SHARES THAT SHE STILL GOES TO MEETINGS AFTER 20-SOME YEARS BECAUSE SHE'S YET TO SEE A NEWCOMER WALK BY THE COUCH IN HER LIVING ROOM."

—ED L., Wrightwood, Calif., Feb 2012

"I prefer night meetings."

ERIC P.

OLDIES BUT GOODIES

The speaker at the Convention's big meeting walked up to the podium, looked out at the stadium full of people and said, "My heart is beating, my knees are weak and my stomach is in knots. I used to pay a lot of money for this feeling."

—CHRISTINE H., Mich., March 2012

MEETINGS IN HELL

I don't know whether there is a heaven or hell, but I am certain that if there is, there will be AA meetings in both places. The only difference will be that in hell, there will be advice-giving and cross talk!

—TERI H., Bloomfield, Conn., Oct 2012

DREAM ON

I was at my Tuesday men's stag meeting celebrating my AA birthday with my wife recently. While we were waiting for the cake to be brought out, I turned to her and said, "Honey, did you ever in your wildest dreams think you'd be standing here helping me celebrate 48 years of sobriety?"

She turned to me and said, "Bruce, let me tell you something. You're not in my wildest dreams!"

—BRUCE D., Manhattan Beach, Calif., Oct 2013

"And there I was, hanging out with the sharks, and I thought this was normal behavior."

NICE TRANSLATION

The man chairing the meeting called on a younger member to share.

She said, "Oh, I've had a terrible day. I wasn't centered. I felt alienated. My child within was deprived. I wasn't self-actualized at all!"

An old-timer who was hard of hearing leaned over and whispered to a friend, "What did she say?"

The friend replied, "She says she's hungry, angry, lonely and tired."

—JOE R., St. James, N.Y., March 2012

WHO'S FROM OUTER SPACE?

A Martian landed at an AA meeting, looked around and said, "Take me to your leader!" Just then, a newcomer turned to him and said, "Hey, you're in the right place, buddy. I said the same thing last week."

—WILL H., Los Angeles, Calif., April 2017

"Congratulations, we're making you our new treasurer. Now, place your left hand on the Big Book, raise your right, and repeat after me..."

ANYBODY, ANYWHERE, AT ANY TIME, CAN JOIN ALCOHOLICS ANONYMOUS. BUT TO JOIN AL-ANON, YOU'VE GOT TO KNOW SOMEONE.

—CHRISTIAN N., Pueblo, Colo., March 2015

OLDIE BUT GOODIE

"I really want to thank you for sticking with me through all the years of drinking and the first five years of my sobriety," said the AA member to her spouse on her fifth-year anniversary. "But I'm curious. If I started drinking again, would you still love me?"

After pondering the question for about a tenth of a second, her husband said, "Of course I'd still love you. I'd miss you, but I'd still love you!"

—RICHARD M., Golden, Colo., April 2016

"Soon I was flying head-on into asteroid belts and abducting earthlings on a daily basis."

GATE CRASHERS

One day, a good man died and went to heaven. He was met at the pearly gates by St. Peter, who escorted him around to the various rooms to see which one he would choose for his eternal dwelling. The first one contained robed saints sitting in a circle repeating chants. "Too spooky," said the man.

The next room held saints shouting, "Hallelujah," and rolling around the floor, while a man screamed from a podium. "Too wild," said the man.

The third one contained prayerful, solemn saints in formal attire counting beads. "Too boring," said the good man.

The final room contained a group of laughing people in worldly attire, using off-color language, smoking cigarettes and drinking coffee. "Who are these people?" asked the man.

"We're not sure," replied St. Peter. "They declare they are not saints, but we let them stay anyway because they've promised they will stay only one day at a time."

—LES B. AND DAVE C., Springfield, Mo., May 2012

"I vote we change this to a discussion meeting!"

IN ORDER TO APOLOGIZE...

An old-timer was going off in a meeting, explaining how the Steps were numbered because they are meant to be worked in order. He went on to say that you can't skip ahead because that would be a formula for disaster.

A newcomer carrying a pot of coffee was so captivated by the old-timer's narrative that she didn't watch where she was going and tripped. She accidentally spilled some of the hot coffee on the old-timer.

Aghast, she stood there in horror as the old-timer wailed at her, saying, "Aren't you even going to say you're sorry?"

Stunned, the newcomer replied, "I would, but I'm not on Step Ten yet!"

—JOHN D., St. Cloud, Minn., Jan 2015

CINDERELLA QUALIFIES

"Did I care if the clock struck midnight? Noooo!"

"OK, this time I'll be the speaker, you be the chairman, and he'll be the new guy."

A MATHEMATICIAN QUALIFIES

"Of course I knew two vector spaces of the same dimension are isomorphic, but did I care?"

THE INVISIBLE MAN QUALIFIES

"Anonymity has never been a problem for me."

ERIC P.

"This is where some of our old-timers sit."

"Sorry ladies, this is strictly a men's meeting."

JOHN B.

ERIC P.

"Doctor Bob comes down and says, 'I've got some good news and some bad news. Good news is I got him down to twelve, the bad news is Direct Amends is still in.'"

TONIGHT'S SPEAKER

One Saturday night, an AA speaker got up to tell his story...

"I graduated from Harvard Law School," he told the crowd. "I was appointed Ambassador to China, was awarded the Nobel Peace Prize for my diplomacy, and then the Pulitzer Prize for my book."

There were two old-timers in the back row and one leaned over and said to the other, "By golly, now we got somebody."

Then the speaker continued, "...then I joined AA and my sponsor told me to quit telling lies."

—HARRY B., Leland, Miss., Jan 2017

"Where exactly is this speaking commitment?"

TIME OUT

A member was asked to speak at a new meeting and got a little carried away. After talking for nearly two hours, he finally realized what he was doing and said, "I'm sorry I talked so long. You see, I left my watch at home."

An old-timer in the back of the room hollered out, "There's a calendar behind you!"

—O.P., Amherst, Nova Scotia, April 2017

LOW TECH

BEFORE I GOT TO AA, I DIDN'T HAVE A PC OR A CELLPHONE. ALL I HAD WAS THE DTs IN A JAIL CELL.

—ROGER S., Redwood City, Calif., Dec 2016

JOHN B.

"Where the %#!! is the power source?"*

KEEP COMING BACK

Twenty-five years ago, I was eager for my husband-to-be (a normie) to understand AA, so I took him to some open meetings, an experience that not many people get to have in their everyday lives.

Later he was describing us to some of his normie friends: "There's usually a speaker and lots of laughing and clapping," he said. "At the end they all hold hands and pray, and then they say, 'Keep coming back. If it works, it works.'"

KAY K., Redondo Beach, Calif., Nov 2015

"He's been puting out the ashtrays for thirty years. We don't have the heart to tell him we've been non-smoking for the last five."

CHAPTER 2

SPONSORSHIP

HEARD AT A MEETING

"I'M A REBEL WITHOUT A CAUSE,"
I TOLD MY SPONSOR.

"NO," HE REPLIED, "YOU'RE A
REBEL WITHOUT A CLUE."

—ANONYMOUS, Aug 2017

"I want to conference my sponsor in on this real quick."

NOT WHAT I HAD IN MIND

A sponsor walked into a meeting one evening to see his sponsee reading the Big Book. "I'm happy to see you reading the book, Joe," the sponsor said. "I'm looking for loopholes," Joe responded.

—BOB M., Green Valley, Ariz., March 2015

"I WAS ON A PINK CLOUD WHEN I FIRST GOT HERE. THEN I MET MY SPONSOR!"

—KAY K., Redondo Beache, Calif., Aug 2013

"Can't start a Fourth Step without a spark, this sponsor's for hire..."

HOW MANY SPONSEES?

AFTER 30 YEARS OF SOBRIETY, I'M OFTEN ASKED BY NEWCOMERS HOW MANY PEOPLE I SPONSOR.

THE ANSWER IS ALWAYS THE SAME: "ABOUT HALF OF THEM."

—JIM K., Beaver Falls, Pa., Oct 2017

"I guess some guys just aren't cut out to be sponsors."

"MY SPONSOR GAVE ME A REALITY CHECK—BUT IT BOUNCED."

—RICHARD M., Golden, Colo., Jan 2012

MAKE THAT CALL!

SPONSOR: "I haven't heard from you in over a month. Don't you know that alcoholism requires daily work on your program? What's your excuse?"

SPONSEE: "I was just doing what you told me."

SPONSOR: "What are you talking about? I told you to keep in touch."

SPONSEE: "You told me to work the Steps every day and to avoid people who irritate me."

—BOB M., Green Valley, Ariz., Nov 2012

"Do you have some time to go over my inventory?"

BITE-SIZED

An angry newcomer was feeling ill and went to the doctor. The doc examined him and backed away, saying, "I'm sorry to tell you this, but you have an advanced case of highly infectious rabies. It will almost certainly be fatal."

Immediately, the newcomer drove over to his sponsor's house and knocked on the door. "Could you give me a pen and paper?" he asked his sponsor. "Do you want to write your Eighth Step list?" asked the sponsor.

"No," the newcomer said, "I want to make a list of all the people I want to bite."

—BOB M., Green Valley, Ariz., Dec 2014

"My sponsor says I shouldn't make any major changes in my first year."

"MY SPONSOR TOLD ME NOT TO PICK UP THE FIRST THINK."

—LUKE A., Trappist, Ky., March 2014

THE BREATHALYZER

When I first came around, I told my sponsor that I drank vodka because you couldn't smell it on my breath, and that I ate mints just in case.

My sponsor asked me if I knew what vodka and breath mints smelled like. I said, "No, what?" He said, "vodka and breath mints."

—KEN K., Lowell, Mich., April 2015

"Sure I ate my sponsor, but did I drink over it?...Noooo!"

VINTAGE NEWCOMER

Q: WHAT'S AN AA NEWCOMER'S FAVORITE WINE?

A: UGH, I HAVE TO CALL MY SPONSOR EVERY DAY?

—WILL H., Los Angeles, Calif., March 2017

"That's my sponsor. We're on Step Three."

41

SPONSOR SCREAMING TO SPONSEE:

"HOW CAN YOU BE SO STUPID? HAVEN'T I TAUGHT YOU EVERYTHING I KNOW?"

—TED U., Bernalillo, N.M., Jan 2016

A SPONSOR'S WISH

A sponsor and sponsee are talking in the parking lot of a meeting:

SPONSOR: "I'm happy to be your sponsor. I wish I had one or two more sponsees like you."

SPONSEE: "Gosh, that's nice to hear. I argue with you all the time and mostly refuse to do most of the things you suggest."

SPONSOR: "Yeah, but I still wish I had one or two more like you. The problem is that I have six!"

—BOB M., Green Valley, Ariz., July 2017

"Don't be silly! My sponsor knows I'm on a date and she's perfectly fine with it!"

THE BEST SPONSOR

My husband was thrilled when I told him I found a sponsor. He had heard how much success there is for alcoholics who have sponsorship. But he got discouraged after our first week of working together and now wants me to fire her. He came home and none of the household chores were done, I was still in my pajamas, and again dinner was not prepared. When he questioned my new lack of participation I simply explained the homework she gave me: "She said I have to change my old ways of thinking, and that I need to stop doing things that I used to do. So honey, I quit. Isn't she amazing?"

—LYNN N., Broken Arrow, Okla., Jan 2014

"Take me to your sponsor..."

45

"It was my sponsor's idea. He suggested I grow a pear."

"Congratulations Janet, you've been added to my Hall of Sponsors."

47

CRASH LANDING

SPONSEE: "I THINK I'VE BEEN CATAPULTED INTO THE FOURTH DIMENSION."

SPONSOR: "NO, YOU'VE JUST HAD TOO MUCH COFFEE."

—JOE M., Sandusky, Ohio, Nov 2017

"I'll have my sponsor call your sponsor."

49

CHAPTER 3

DATING & MARRIAGE

JUST CHECKING

A tipsy gentleman in a great-looking suit—with his hair well-groomed, a flower in his lapel and smelling like a good aftershave—walks into an upscale cocktail lounge. He sees a woman seated at the bar and walks over, sits beside her and orders a drink. He takes a sip, turns to her and says, "So tell me, do I come here often?"

—BOB M., Green Valley, Ariz., Sept 2017

NO CINDERELLA

SOBRIETY IS NEVER HAVING TO SAY, "HEY, WHAT'S YOUR NAME? CAN YOU HELP ME FIND MY OTHER SHOE?"

—PATRICK M., Pittsburgh, Pa., Nov 2017

"Honey, I've got a year now...can't we lose the chalk-line?"

CAN'T WIN

Mike had not been communicating well with his wife lately, so he asked his buddy at work, Bill, how things were going at his house. Bill replied, "Fantastic! I give her a hug and a kiss when I go home. I tell her she looks good, and I compliment her on her cooking. She really appreciates all the attention I give her."

So Mike thought he'd give it a go. When he got home, he gave his wife a huge hug, kissed her, and told her that he loved her. His wife burst into tears. Mike was confused and asked why she was crying.

She said, "This is the worst day of my life. First, little Billy fell off his bike and twisted his ankle. Then, the washing machine broke and flooded the basement. And now, you come home drunk!"

—RICHARD M., Golden, Colo., Feb 2013

"It's official! I can fish sober!"

JOHN B.

DOUBLE TROUBLE

A drunk stumbles up to the only other patron in a bar and asks if he can buy him a drink. "Why, of course," the guy replies.

Drunk 1: "Where are you from?"

Drunk 2: "I'm from Ireland."

Drunk 1: "Hey, I'm from Ireland too. Let's have another round to Ireland!" Then with a curious look, he asks, "Where in Ireland?"

Drunk 2: "Why, Dublin!"

Drunk 1: "I can't believe it, me too! Let's have a round for Dublin!"

Drunk 2: "Of course! Hey, what school did you go to?"

Drunk 1: "Saint Mary's. I graduated in '62."

Then both drunks yell in unison: "Me too! This is unbelievable!"

About that time, one of the regulars strolls in and sits down at the bar. "What's up?" he asks the bartender. "Oh, nothing much," replies the bartender. "The O'Malley twins are drunk again."

—ANONYMOUS, June 2015

"If I had been as picky choosing a husband as I am choosing
a sponsor, I'd still be married!"

A COLD WIFE

I just got off the phone with a friend who lives in North Dakota. She said that since early this morning the snow has been nearly waist high, and it's still falling. The temperature is 32 below zero, and the north wind is increasing to near gale force. Her husband has done nothing but look through the kitchen window and just stare. She says if it gets much worse, she may have to let the drunken bum in.

—DICK S., Shrewsbury, Pa., May 2014

TEXT TO WIFE:

MARY, HAVING ONE MORE PINT WITH THE LADS. IF NOT HOME IN 20 MINUTES, READ THIS MESSAGE AGAIN.

—BILL B., Oakland, Fla., April 2014

"Honey, I wantcha to meet a friend of mine..."

UNDER COVER

MIKE TO CHARLIE THE BARTENDER: "POUR ME A STIFF ONE, CHARLIE. I JUST HAD ANOTHER FIGHT WITH THE LITTLE WOMAN."

CHARLIE: "OH YEAH? AND HOW DID THIS ONE END?"

MIKE: "SHE CAME TO ME ON HER HANDS AND KNEES."

CHARLIE: "REALLY? THAT'S A SWITCH. WHAT DID SHE SAY?"

MIKE: "SHE SAID, 'COME OUT FROM UNDER THAT BED, YOU GUTLESS WONDER!'"

—Will N., Arlington Heights, Ill., Aug 2014

"Whaddaya say we go somewhere cozy and tell each other the exact nature of our wrongs?"

DOCTOR'S ORDERS

A doctor told Mrs. McMurphy to give her husband one pill a day and one drink of whiskey to improve his stamina.

A month later, when Mrs. McMurphy came in for another visit, the doctor asked, "How are we doing with the pill and the whiskey?"

"Well, he's a little behind with the pills," she answered, "but he's about six years ahead with the whiskey."

—BOB M., Green Valley, Ariz., Aug 2016

TRUE LOVE

AA ROMANCE: SHE MET HIM ONLINE. HE SAID HE LIVED IN A GATED COMMUNITY. HE WAS BEING HONEST. HE WAS IN STATE PRISON.

—JIMMY, Prescott, Ariz., April 2017

"Come in...we're celebrating John's 40th year of low self-esteem."

REJECTED AGAIN

I was at a party with sober friends when I met this attractive woman who seemed interested in me, so I asked her out. She politely shrugged and said, "No thanks," which really surprised me.

I asked, "Why, is it my age?" She replied, "No, age doesn't matter."

"Well then," I asked, "is it my religion?" She said, "No, religion doesn't matter either."

Bewildered, I asked, "I don't get it, is it because you're married?" She replied, "No, I'm single."

I was totally perplexed. So I said, "I'm confused. Why won't you go out with me? Is it because I'm sober?"

"No," she said, "it's because I'm sober!"

—KENNY B., Kailua, Hawaii, Aug 2013

JOHN B.

"Tell me again about how you intuitively handle situations that used to baffle you..."

HOW DID YOU DO THAT?

A drunk went to a police station wanting to speak with the burglar who had broken into his house the night before. "You'll get your chance in court," said the desk sergeant.

"No, no, no!" said the man. "I want to know how he got into the house without waking my wife. I've been trying to do that for years!"

—BOB M., Green Valley, Ariz., Jan 2012

OLDIE BUT GOODIE

A badly hungover husband sat at the breakfast table, his eyes half shut and his tongue feeling as though he had been licking a dusty rug.

Moodily toying with his food, he complained, "These eggs taste funny."

"Of course your eggs taste funny," snapped his spouse. "They're pancakes."

—ANONYMOUS, Aug 2016

"He's having trouble working the steps..."

CAN'T GET PASTOR

A MINISTER DRIVES BY A TAVERN AS BOB AND LARRY ARE SNEAKING A BEER.

BOB: "I HOPE THE REVEREND DIDN'T SEE US."

LARRY: "WHO CARES...GOD'S THE ONLY ONE WHO COUNTS."

BOB: "YEAH, BUT GOD WON'T TELL MY WIFE."

—TERRY B., May 2013

"I'm sure we've met before...was it at Dolan's Drunk Farm or
the State Hospital?"

UH, THANKS DOC

Herb went to the doctor for a routine exam. While he was there, he told the doctor that he wasn't able to do all the things around the house that he used to do. "Cuz I'm usually pretty drunk when I get home," he explained.

When the examination was complete, Herb looked at the doctor and said, "Now Doc, I can take it. Tell me in plain English what's wrong with me."

"Well, in plain English," the doctor replied, "you're just a lazy old drunk."

"OK," said Herb. "Now give me the Latin term, so I can tell my wife."

—BOB M., Green Valley, Ariz., Dec 2017

"Sorry lady, it doesn't work that way."

JOHN B.

DOUBLE DILEMMA

A NEWCOMER TOLD HIS SPONSOR THAT HE WAS ENGAGED IN A MAJOR CUSTODY BATTLE. **HIS WIFE DOESN'T WANT HIM . . . AND HIS MOTHER WON'T TAKE HIM BACK!**

—BOB M., Green Valley, Ariz., July 2016

THE HITCHHIKER

A slick city man driving past a small town picked up a drunken hitchhiker. As they were driving along, the drunk noticed a brown paper bag on the dashboard and inquired as to its contents. The city man replied, "It's a bottle of wine. I got it for my wife." The drunk, looking pensively down the road, nodded his head solemnly and said, "Good trade."

—BRAD U., Cheshire, Conn., Aug 2015

"This too shall pass..."

HAPPY ANNIVERSARY, DEAR

A remorseful drunk comes to one morning and realizes it's his 20th wedding anniversary. He rolls over and says to his wife, "Happy 20th anniversary dear. I'm going to get you a real nice present today."

She gives him a look. "The only thing I want is a divorce," she says.

A bit amazed, he thinks for a moment and replies, "I wasn't planning on spending that much."

—JOHN H., Council Bluffs, Iowa, Sept 2014

WAS THAT YOU?

Breakfast was a very late affair that day and the husband and wife were fragile indeed—badly hungover from a particularly wild party the night before. Bleary-eyed, with two trembling hands holding his black coffee, our hero asked his wife, "Was it you I made out with in the garden last night?" She struggled to bring him into focus. "About what time?" she replied.

—BOB M., Green Valley, Ariz., May 2012

"And to think of all the holiday fun you missed sitting in the bar!"

PARTNERS FOR LIFE

AT A SCOTTISH WEDDING RECEPTION THE D.J. YELLED, "WOULD ALL MARRIED MEN PLEASE STAND NEXT TO THE ONE PERSON WHO HAS MADE YOUR LIFE WORTH LIVING." **THE BARTENDER WAS ALMOST CRUSHED TO DEATH.**

—ROGER B., Santa Rosa, Calif., Sept 2013

CHAPTER 4

FRIENDS, FAMILY, COWORKERS

WHAT'S THE USE?

A drunk had been sitting at a bar most of the day and had passed out. His buddies rubbed a wedge of limburger cheese on his upper lip. After a while, his nose began to twitch, his eyes opened, he sniffed and declared, "Wow, this place really stinks!" Then he ran outside. Several minutes later, he returned dejectedly, saying, "Give me a drink. It's no use. The whole world stinks!"

—CHUCK M., Freehold, N.J., June 2012

HEARD AT A MEETING

"SOMETIMES I FEEL LIKE A FRUIT LOOP IN A BOWL FULL OF CHEERIOS."

—ED L., Wrightwood, Calif., Nov 2012

"Tonight's story is called 'A Vision for You.'"

BUCKLE UP

An AA was running late driving to work one morning. Noticing that the carpool lane was shorter, she got in it. Soon a police officer came up behind her, turned on his lights and pulled her over. The officer walked up to the car and the woman lowered her window.

"Ma'am," the policeman asked, "do you know why I'm pulling you over?"

"No, sir, I'm afraid that I don't," the woman replied.

"You're in the carpool lane, yet you have no other passenger in your vehicle. Why is this?" he asked.

Thinking quickly, the woman replied, "Well, you see officer, I'm an alcoholic. Prior to recovery, my life had become one of incomprehensible demoralization. Once I became involved in AA, however, I found my Higher Power and began working the Steps and have lived a life better than I could ever have imagined. In gratitude, I take my Higher Power with me wherever I go. So while it appears that I'm riding alone, I really am not."

"I see," replied the officer. He then proceeded to pull out his ticket book and began to write her a ticket.

"But officer, I don't think you understand," she pleaded. "There are two of us in the vehicle."

"Ma'am," replied the officer, "I do understand. You see, I too am a grateful member of AA and I also take my Higher Power with me wherever I go."

"Then, why the ticket?" she asked.

"Because your Higher Power isn't wearing a seat belt," he said.

—CHRIS B., West Bend, Wis., May 2015

"*Joining AA was an excellent move Fenton, but let's not overdo the 'Easy Does It' part.*"

MEMORY LAME

Three women friends were sitting around the kitchen table doing what they enjoyed—drinking beer by the case. One woman said, "I wonder if all this beer is affecting my memory. This afternoon I saw an open jar of mayonnaise on the counter and I couldn't remember if I had finished a sandwich and hadn't put the jar away, or if it was out because I was going to make a sandwich." "I know what you mean," the second woman said. "Yesterday, I found myself in the middle of the stairs and couldn't remember if I was going up or down." "Well, I've had as much beer as either of you," the third woman said, "and I've never had any memory problems. And I hope I never will." With that, she reached over and quickly knocked on the wooden table three times. "Oh," she exclaimed, "somebody's at the door. I'll get it!"

—DUSTY B., Hancock, Maine, July 2018

"*How long have I been making the coffee? Since the night I complained about it....Why, you got a problem with it?*"

GEE, THANKS MOM!

Wino 1: "I had the greatest dream last night!"

Wino 2: "What happened?"

Wino 1: "I was at my mama's and she got me a ticket to Disneyland. I went on all the rides, saw the dancing characters, saw Mickey and Minnie Mouse—I had the best time!"

Wino 2: "I had a great dream too! I dreamt I was living in a first-class penthouse, I had a case of top-shelf whiskey, and then two beautiful women came over!"

Wino 1: "Man, why didn't you call me?!"

Wino 2: "I did, but your mama said you were at Disneyland."

—JENNIFER R., Boulder, Colo., Jan 2012

ONE TOO MANY

MY WIFE THINKS I'M TOO DRUNK TO TAKE THE GOLDFISH OUT FOR A WALK. I'LL SHOW HER!

—DAVID M., Oswego, N.Y., June 2017

"You have a rare form of paranoia...you think everybody likes you."

LOUD AND CLEAR

THREE RETIREES, EACH WITH HEARING LOSS, WERE PLAYING GOLF ONE BEAUTIFUL DAY. ONE GUY REMARKED TO THE OTHER, "WINDY, ISN'T IT?" "NO," THE SECOND MAN, REPLIED, "IT'S THURSDAY." THE THIRD MAN CHIMED IN, "SO AM I. LET'S GO HAVE A BEER!"

—BOB M., Green Valley, Ariz., Nov 2013

"Why does it not surprise me? The dog's higher on his amends list than I am."

THE SENSIBLE ONE

Robert and his buddy Fred were getting drunk at their favorite bar. Joe walked in and joined them. Right away, Joe began chugging down one drink after another. In just a short time, Joe passed out and fell on the floor. As he lay there all sprawled out, Robert said to Fred, "That's what I like about Joe. He always knows when to quit."

—DUSTY B., Hancock, Maine, Aug 2018

HEARD AT A MEETING

"I CAME INTO AA WITH BACK PROBLEMS. **MY WIFE WAS ON MY BACK.** THE JUDGE WAS ON MY BACK. AND MY EMPLOYER WAS ON MY BACK!"

—DANIEL B., March 2015

"I never wanted to be a worker among workers."

FIGHTIN' WORDS

A drunk stumbles into a biker bar and orders a drink. He sees three men sitting at a corner table, so he staggers over and looks the biggest, meanest biker in the face and says, "I was at your grandma's house today, and man, she is one fine-looking woman!"

The biker doesn't say a word. His buddies are confused, because he's one bad biker and would fight at the drop of a hat. The drunk leans over again and says, "I made out with your grandma and she's the best kisser I ever met." The biker's buddies are starting to get mad but the biker still says nothing.

The drunk leans on the table one more time and says, "I'll tell you something else, boy, your grandma really liked it!"

At this point the biker stands up, takes the drunk by the shoulders looks him square in the eye and says, "Grandpa, go home!"

—BOB M., Green Valley, Ariz., Feb 2014

"I know Rover's glad Ralph got sober...he's finally got his house all to himself."

OLDIE BUT GOODIE

The town drunk went to see the doctor. "My whole body hurts," he complained. The drunk put his finger on his left shoulder. "When I touch myself here, it hurts," he whined. Then he put his finger near his heart. "When I touch myself here, it hurts," he said. Then he put his finger on his thigh, moaned and said, "When I touch myself here, it hurts too. No matter where I touch myself, Doc, it hurts something terrible! Please, tell me what's wrong with me."

The doctor replied, "You have a broken finger."

—ANONYMOUS, New York, N.Y., Oct 2018

SENILITY PRAYER

GOD GRANT ME THE SENILITY TO FORGET THE PEOPLE I NEVER LIKED ANYWAY, THE GOOD FORTUNE TO RUN INTO THE ONES I DO, **AND THE EYESIGHT TO TELL THE DIFFERENCE.**

—DAN H., Davie, Fla., Dec 2013

"I feel like I don't fit in."

"The old-timers are at it again...arguing over who's got the most serenity."

JOHN B.

FAMILY HOLIDAY

The entire family gathered for the big holiday dinner, including the drunken uncle who put in his usual annual appearance. During dinner, his 4-year-old niece kept staring at him. He checked his tie, felt his face for food and patted his hair in place, but nothing stopped her from staring at him. The uncle tried his best to just ignore her, but finally it was too much for him. "Why are you staring at me?" he asked her. Everyone at the table had noticed this and all conversation stopped to await her response. The little girl said, "They all said you drink like a fish. I just wanted to see how you did that."

—PAUL C., Oceanside, Calif., Dec 2015

COURT ORDER
A DRUNK WAS ARRESTED AND BROUGHT IN FRONT OF A JUDGE. JUDGE: "SIR, YOU'VE BEEN BROUGHT HERE FOR DRINKING." DRUNK: "OK, JUDGE, LET'S GET STARTED."

—STUART S., Alexandria, Va., Jan 2015

"Humility? I'm all about humility. I'm the most humble person on the planet."

ERIC P.

THE PARKING GOD

An alcoholic was late for his court appearance and he was circling the courthouse, desperately looking for a parking spot. Finally, out of desperation he looked up and said, "God please let me find a spot to park and I swear I'll never drink again!" Right then someone pulled out right in front of him, and he happily parked. The guy got out of his car and looked up and said, "Never mind, I found one myself."

—JOHN L., Woonsocket, R.I., Jan 2017

SAIL AWAY

"How long have you been driving without a tail light?" asked the policeman after pulling over a motorist.

The driver leaped out of his car, ran to the back and gave a long, painful groan and put his face in his hands. He seemed so upset that the cop was moved to ease up on him a bit.

"Come on, now," the policeman said, "you don't have to take it so hard. It isn't that serious."

"It isn't?" cried the motorist. "Then you know what happened to my boat trailer and my six cases of beer in the boat?"

—BOB M., Green Valley, Ariz., Feb 2017

"I didn't care what litter box I woke up in."

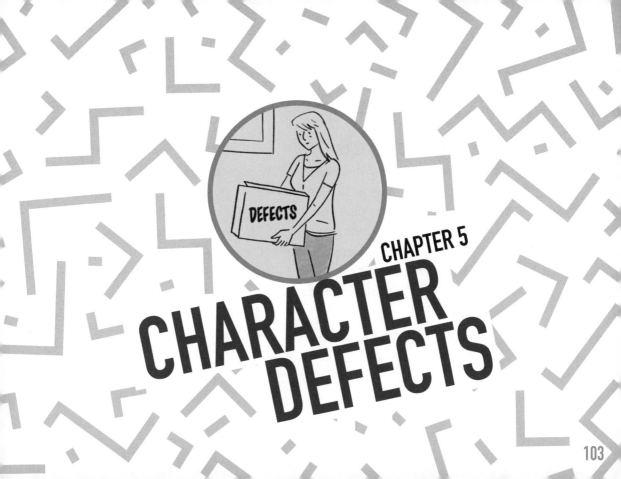

CHAPTER 5

CHARACTER DEFECTS

A DAY AT THE GROCERY STORE

A drunk dad goes to the supermarket and notices a woman waving at him. She says hello. He's rather taken aback because he can't place where he knows her from. "Do you know me?" he asks. She replies, "I think that you're the father of one of my kids." He thinks for a moment, then says, "Oh my gosh, are you the stripper from my bachelor party? I was pretty drunk that night!" She looks into his eyes and says calmly, "No, I'm your son's teacher."

—BOB M., Green Valley, Ariz., April 2018

WORLDS LONGEST FOURTH STEP

HIS NEW BEST FRIEND

An alcoholic had just gotten a divorce, lost his children, been fired from his job and was facing eviction when he noticed a case of beer bottles in his trash. He took out an empty bottle, smashed it and swore, "You're why I don't have a wife!" He threw a second bottle and said, "You're why I don't have my children!" Then a third..."You're why I lost my job!" Then he discovered a fourth bottle, still sealed and full of beer. He took it, tucked it into his pocket, and said, "Stand aside, my friend—I know you were not involved."

—TONY W., Fairfield, Calif., Oct 2012

BAD INVESTMENT

Q: HOW DO YOU TURN AN ALCOHOLIC INTO A MILLIONAIRE?

A: GIVE HIM A BILLION DOLLARS.

—J.D., Big Lake, Minn., Sept 2015

"Thanks, but being sober is outside my comfort zone."

EARLY BIRD PRAYER

Dear Higher Power, so far today
I've done all right. I haven't gossiped, lost my temper, been greedy,
grumpy, nasty, selfish or overindulgent. I'm very thankful for the kind
of day you have given me. But in
a few minutes, Higher Power, I'm
going to get out of bed, and from
then on I'm going to need a lot more
help! Amen.

—JOHN H., Council Bluffs, Iowa, April 2016

CRASH LANDING

A few months before I joined AA,
I went on a terrific blackout drunk
the night before I was to catch an
early-morning flight. My gait was
still unsteady as I boarded. Yes, I
was weaving on a jet plane.

—Paul C., Oceanside, Calif., Jan 2019

DARTH VADER'S FIFTH STEP

"I pulverized planet Alderaan, tried to lure my son to the Dark Side, destroyed Garrison Moon of Kessel..."

CRYSTAL CLEAR

When I was drinking, I was in denial about almost everything. And what I wasn't in denial about, I was deluded over. Here's the difference between denial and delusion:

Denial is when you tell yourself, "There's nothing wrong with my relationship, it's all good," when actually your relationship is very dysfunctional.

Delusion is when you tell yourself, "There's nothing wrong with my relationship, it's all good"…and you're no longer in one.

—JAMES G., Santa Rosa, Calif., Sept 2017

HEARD AT A MEETING

"AS A NEWCOMER, I SOUNDED LIKE I COULD DO FOR GOD WHAT GOD COULDN'T DO FOR HIMSELF."

—ED L., Wrightwood, Calif., June 2017

"It's like one is too many and a thousand is not enough."

EDDIE E.

111

HEARD AT A MEETING

Despite sometimes having an arrogant exterior, an alcoholic is very much capable of such feelings as love, affection, intimacy and caring. However, these feelings don't usually involve anyone else.

—BOB M., Green Valley, Ariz., May 2014

UNPLUGGED

When I was first sober, I bought a universal remote control for my home entertainment system. You can imagine my disappointment when I found that I still could not control the universe.

—DAVE C., Burley, Idaho, Nov 2014

"I told you you'd get your brains back after five years."

QUIET PLEASE

A drunk goes up to the counter and shouts, "Hey! Can I have a cheeseburger and fries?"

The woman at the counter quickly replies, "Sir, this is a library."

"Oh, sorry," the drunk whispers, "can I have a cheeseburger and fries?"

—AMARDEEP S., Brooklyn, N.Y., May 2018

OUT OF TIME

A man walks into an antique store and buys a grandfather clock. As he carries it out of the shop, he accidentally crashes into a drunk and they both fall over, smashing the clock to bits.

The man looks at the drunk and says, "Why don't you look where you're going?" The drunk replies, "Why don't you wear a watch like everybody else?"

—IVOR D., Puyallup, Wash., March 2016

WHISKEY DIET

A DRUNK WAS SITTING AT THE BAR BRAGGING TO HIS BUDDY. "I'VE BEEN ON THE WHISKEY DIET," HE SAID. "OH YEAH?" HIS BUDDY REPLIED. "YEAH," SAID THE DRUNK. "I'VE LOST THREE DAYS ALREADY!"

—DEANNA S., Alpharetta, Ga., Oct 2017

"Yeah, I was gonna hang on to those."

CAUGHT ON TAPE

DEAR ALCOHOL, WE HAD A DEAL. YOU WERE GOING TO MAKE ME FUNNIER, SEXIER, MORE INTELLIGENT AND A BETTER DANCER. **I SAW THE VIDEO. WE NEED TO TALK.**

—ANONYMOUS, Jan 2014

"After I stomped Tokyo, I went after this tiny fishing village..."

117

I WOULDN'T LIE

A problem drinker was flat broke, so she went to her landlord and said, "I'm sorry, but I can't pay my rent this month."

"Listen," the owner replied, "you told me the same thing last month and the month before."

"Sure," answered the lush. "And didn't I keep my word?"

—BOB M., Green Valley, Ariz., Jan 2014

BETTER DAYS

I thought I had bad days, but now I've learned that I have bad moments for five minutes and complain about it the whole day.

—ANONYMOUS, April 2014

DOGHOUSE

WHAT'S THE DIFFERENCE BETWEEN AN ALCOHOLIC AND A DOG? **THE DOG STOPS WHINING AFTER YOU LET IT BACK IN THE HOUSE!**

—ED L., Wrightwood, Calif., Feb 2015

"Oh, we're not here to do MY Fifth Step..."

HEARD AT A MEETING

"I PRACTICE MY OPINION IN ALL MY AFFAIRS."

—ED L. Wrightwood, Calif., Dec 2015

SHALL WE GATHER

One morning, a preacher was completing his temperance sermon. With great expression, he exclaimed, "If I had all the beer in the world, I'd take it and throw it into the river!" With even greater emphasis he added, "And if I had all the wine in the world, I'd take it and throw it into the river!"

Then the preacher closed his sermon with this: "And if I had all the whiskey in the world, I'd take it and throw it into the river!" When he was done, he sat down. The leader of the chorus then stood very cautiously and announced with a big smile, "For our clo-sching schong, let ussch sching hymn number 365, 'Schall We Gather at the River.'"

—BOB M., Green Valley, Ariz., Aug 2018

"I humbly asked Him to remove my shortcomings, but he left a few."

ERIC P.

HARD TO SAY

WORDS THAT ARE DIFFICULT TO SAY
WHEN DRUNK:

1. Innovative
2. Preliminary
3. Proliferation
4. Cinnamon

WORDS THAT ARE VERY DIFFICULT
TO SAY WHEN DRUNK:

1. Specificity
2. Anti-constitutionality
3. Passive-aggressive disorder
4. Transubstantiate

WORDS THAT ARE DOWNRIGHT IM-
POSSIBLE TO SAY WHEN DRUNK:

1. No thanks, I'm married.
2. Nope, no more booze for me!

3. Sorry, but you're not really my type.

4. No thanks, I'm not hungry.

5. I'm not interested in fighting you.

6. Thank you, but I won't make any attempt to dance. I have no coordination and would hate to look like a real fool!

7. Oh no, I must be going home now as I have to work in the morning.

—WILL N., Arlington Heights, Ill., March 2013

"Hey fella, you ready to hear another Fifth Step?"

IT'S A MIRACLE

A pastor is stumbling across a parking lot looking for his car, when a cop sees him. The officer walks up to him and asks, "Have you had anything to drink tonight sir?"

"No," the pastor replies.

"So, what's in that cup?" the cop asks.

"Water sir, take a look!" he says.

Looking in the cup, the officer says, "This isn't water, it's wine!"

Gasping, the pastor exclaims, "He did it again!"

—BARRY O., Albuquerque, N.M., June 2015

THE "I"S HAVE IT

THE REASON TWO ALCOHOLICS CAN'T COMMUNICATE EFFECTIVELY WITH EACH OTHER IS THAT WHEN THEY TALK, IT'S ALWAYS "AN I FOR AN I."

—Richard M., Golden, Colo., June 2013

SLOW EARNER

WHAT'S THE DIFFERENCE BETWEEN A DRUNK AND A SAVINGS BOND?

WELL, THE SAVINGS BOND EVENTUALLY MATURES…AND EARNS MONEY.

—LARRY R., Milwaukee, Wis., Jan 2018

UNIVERSAL PROBLEM

An alcoholic had an appointment to see a new psychiatrist for the first time.

When the patient was settled comfortably on the couch, the psychiatrist began his therapy session.

"What seems to be your problem?" the doctor asked. "Perhaps you should start at the very beginning."

"Of course," the alcoholic replied. "In the beginning, I created the heavens and the earth…"

—BOB M., Green Valley, Ariz., Feb 2018

HARDHEADED

An alcoholic goes to confession one Sunday morning and says to the priest, "Forgive me Father, for I have sinned."

The priest asks, "What have you done my son?"

The alcoholic replies, "I stole 50 sheets of plywood."

The priest responds, "You are forgiven, now go and steal no more."

Next week the alcoholic comes back to the same priest and confesses the very same sin!

The priest asks, "Didn't I tell you to go and steal no more? This time you must make an amends for stealing. You do know how to make an amends, don't you?"

The alcoholic replies, "No, but if you can get the blueprints, I can get the plywood!"

—DENNIS S., Harper's Ferry, W.V., Oct 2013

"I had a low bottom."

129

CHAPTER 6

GOTTA LOVE AA

OBSTACLE COURSE

Q: How do you know when you're too drunk to drive?

A: When the tree you've been dodging all night turns out to be the air freshener hanging on your rearview mirror.

—DEBORAH B., Wichita, Kan., Feb 2012

ON THE DOUBLE!

A drunk staggered out of the bar and got into a taxi. He said, "Buddy, take me to Joe's Place." The driver replied, "You are at Joe's Place." So the drunk reached in his pocket, pulled out a $10 bill and said, "Oh alright, but next time don't drive so fast!"

—MARION C., Brunswick, Ga., Oct 2012

HANGOVER MADNESS

I DIDN'T THINK MY HANGOVER WAS THAT BAD UNTIL I SPENT 10 MINUTES TRYING TO LOG ON TO MY KID'S ETCH-A-SKETCH!

—BOB M., Green Valley, Ariz., Oct 2012

"First, explain to me what a 'slip' is."

BE CAREFUL WHAT YOU WISH FOR

A man walks up to the bar with an ostrich behind him, and the bartender asks for their order.

The man says, "I'll have a beer," and turns to the ostrich. "What's yours?" "I'll have a beer too," says the ostrich. The bartender pours the beer and says "That will be $3.40 please," and the man reaches into his pocket and pays with the exact change.

The next day, the man and the ostrich come again. This time the bartender serves them two large scotches, and once again the man pays with exact change.

This becomes a routine, until late one evening the two enter again. This time, the bartender can't hold back his curiosity any longer. "Excuse me, sir," he says. "How do you manage to always come up with the exact change every time?"

"Well," says the man, "several years ago I was cleaning the attic, and I found this old lamp. When I rubbed it a genie appeared and offered me two wishes. My first wish was that if I ever needed to pay for anything, I just put my hand in my pocket and the right amount of money will be there."

"That's brilliant!" says the bartender. "Most people would wish for a million dollars, but you'll always be as rich as you want for as long as you live! You're a genius!"

"Oh, one other thing sir," adds the bartender. "What's with the ostrich?" The man replies, "Oh, my second wish was for a chick with long legs." —MARION C., Brunswick, Ga., April 2013

"Is there alcohol in this?"

BAD HABITS

A drunk staggered out of a bar early one afternoon. He had been drinking since early in the day. As he stumbled down the street, two nuns were coming toward him. He started to tip his hat respectfully to them. But at the same time the nuns went around him—one to his right and the other to his left.

He got a confused look on his face and then slurred, "How the heck did she do that?"

—BOB M., Green Valley, Ariz., May 2013

SECOND OPINION

THE DOCTOR TOLD HIS PATIENT HE WASN'T SURE OF THE DIAGNOSIS, BUT THOUGHT IT COULD BE DUE TO ALCOHOL. THE PATIENT REPLIED, "THAT'S OK, DOC. I'LL COME BACK WHEN YOU'RE SOBER."

—BRIAN M., Feb 2015

"Nobody can light up a birthday party like a drunk."

WEIGHT A MINUTE!

A DRUNK WALKS UP TO A PARKING METER AND PUTS IN SOME CHANGE. THE METER GOES UP TO 60 AND HE TAKES ANOTHER LOOK… **"HEY," HE SAYS, "I LOST 100 POUNDS!"**

—MARION C., Brunswick, Ga., Nov 2013

"At the stroke of midnight you will be visited by three spirits...and if that doesn't work...two guys from AA."

JOHN B.

FILL 'ER UP!

A big, burly man approached the checkout counter of the local liquor store with 10 cases of beer. "My goodness! Do you have a container to carry that out?" asked the clerk. "You're looking at it," replied the customer.

—PAUL C., Oceanside, Calif., Nov 2017

POOR OL' JAKE

Poor ol' Jake was an alcoholic. To make matters worse, he was an agnostic. In addition he was an insomniac, and to top it off, he was dyslexic. Any night of the week you could find him sitting on the corner of his bed sipping whiskey from a coffee mug, and wondering if there really was a Dog.

—E.O., Gatlinburg, Tenn., April 2014

DRUNKEN SAFARI

YOU'RE RIDING A HORSE AT FULL SPEED. THERE'S A GIRAFFE ON YOUR RIGHT, KEEPING UP WITH YOU, AND THERE'S A LION DIRECTLY BEHIND YOU, RIGHT ON YOUR TAIL. WHAT DO YOU DO? GET YOUR DRUNK A— OFF THE CAROUSEL!

—SANDY B., July 2013

"Sure, I'd be happy to explain some of the basic concepts of this program...let's start with anonymity."

BAR BOUNCER

Two drunks are sitting across from a bartender on the second floor of a building. The first drunk says to the second drunk, "I bet I can run over to that open window and jump out and hit the ground and bounce back up here onto this barstool." The second drunk dares him.

So the first guy runs and dives out the window, and sure enough, he bounces off the ground and springs back up onto the bar stool. Then he turns to the second drunk and says, "It's your turn!"

The second guy runs and jumps out the window only to crash on the ground.

While the first drunk is laughing hysterically, the bartender turns to him and says, "You're a cruel man, Clark Kent!"

—JIM R., West Allis, Wis., Feb 2015

"With all due respect Your Honor, if you spot it, you got it."

TAKING A STAND

A drunk named Joe put his shoes on after a long night and a terrible hangover. His wife noticed that his left shoe was on his right foot.

"Joe, your shoes are on the wrong feet," she told him.

He looked up with a puzzled expression and said, "Oh no, honey, these are my feet!"

—BOB M., Green Valley, Ariz., May 2017

MAKING MISTAKES

Q: How do you know when an alcoholic has used a word processor?

A: There's whiteout on the screen.

—STEVE L., Worcester, Mass., June 2017

BLAZING ROAD BLOCK

A juggler driving to his next performance is stopped by the police. "What are these matches and lighter fluid doing in your car?" asks the cop.

"I'm a juggler, and I use flaming torches in my act."

"Oh yeah?" says the doubtful cop. "Let's see you do it." The juggler gets out and starts juggling the blazing torches masterfully.

A couple driving by slows down to watch. "Wow," says the driver to his wife. "I'm glad I quit drinking. Look at the test they're giving now!"

—MARION C., Brunswick, Ga., June 2014

"There's a two drink minimum."

"Don't blame yourself honey, I'm sure there were other reasons than you getting sober."

"That streetlight is 'people, places, and things' for me."

147

TRYING TO MAKE CENTS

My partner told me that we couldn't afford beer anymore, and I'd have to quit. Then I caught her spending $65 on makeup. I asked her why I had to give up stuff and she didn't. She said she needed the makeup to look pretty for me. I told her that was what the beer was for!...I don't think she's coming back.

—MARY B., Menominee, Mich., June 2013

WRECKED

DID YOU HEAR ABOUT THE NEW AUTO INSURANCE PRODUCT FOR ALCOHOLICS? IT'S CALLED "MY FAULT."

—TERRY B., Albany, N.Y., Aug 2016

"I have this sense of impending happiness."

DOCTOR'S ORDERS

A doctor has just finished giving a young man a thorough physical examination.

DOC: The best thing for you to do is give up drinking and smoking, get to bed early and stay away from women.

YOUNG MAN: Hey doc, I don't deserve the best. What's second best?

—BOB M., Green Valley, Ariz., April 2014

A NEW LEAF

I'VE READ SO MANY HORRIBLE THINGS ABOUT DRINKING AND POOR HEALTH RECENTLY THAT I MADE A FIRM NEW YEAR'S RESOLUTION: NO MORE READING!

—D.H., Davie, Fla., April 2018

"Before we start we need to be clear about something..."

WRONG NUMBER

A drunk guy met up with his friend at a bar. The friend noticed that the man had bright red blisters on both ears and asked him what had happened. The drunk responded, "My wife left the iron on. When the phone rang, I picked up the iron by mistake." His friend thought this over and then asked him what happened to his other ear. The drunk responded, "The damn fool called back!"

—TAYLOR O., Lakewood, Colo., July 2018

HEARD AT A MEETING

"I DRANK FOR TWO REASONS: I HAD A MOUTH AND MY ARM BENT AT THE ELBOW."

—ED L., Wrightwood, Calif., Oct 2018

ONE FUR THE ROAD

A PENGUIN AND A SKUNK WALK INTO A BAR. AFTER HAVING SEVERAL ROUNDS, THE SKUNK LOOKS OVER AND ASKS THE PENGUIN, "IS MY SUIT ON BACKWARDS?"

—SARA D., Nine Mile Falls, Wash., Jan 2017

"I think it's time we had a serious discussion about your slogan 'Live and Let Live.'"

WHEN IRISH EYES ARE SMILING

The rain was pouring down. Standing in front of a big puddle outside the pub was an old Irishman, drenched, holding a stick with a piece of string dangling in the water.

A passerby stopped and asked, "What are you doing?"

"Fishing," replied the old man. Feeling sorry for the old man, the gent said, "Come in out of the rain and have a drink with me."

In the warmth of the pub, as they sipped their whiskies, the gentleman, being a bit of a smart aleck, could not resist asking, "So how many have you caught today?"

"You're the eighth," said the old man.

—BOB M., Green Valley, Ariz., June 2018

A THIRSTY MIND

OPTIMIST: "MY GLASS IS HALF FULL." PESSIMIST: "MY GLASS IS HALF EMPTY." ALCOHOLIC: "YOU GONNA FINISH THAT?"

—JIM S., Virginia Beach, Va., Feb 2018

"I call it 'Early Sobriety.'"

EDDIE E.

ALCOHOLICS ANONYMOUS

AA's program of recovery is fully set forth in its basic text, *Alcoholics Anonymous* (commonly known as the Big Book), now in its Fourth Edition, as well as in *Twelve Steps and Twelve Traditions*, *Living Sober*, and other books. Information on AA can also be found on AA's website at www.aa.org, or by writing to:

Alcoholics Anonymous, Box 459
Grand Central Station, New York, NY 10163

For local resources, check your local telephone directory under "Alcoholics Anonymous." Four pamphlets, "This is A.A.," "Is A.A. For You?,"
"44 Questions," and "A Newcomer Asks" are also available from AA.

AA GRAPEVINE

AA Grapevine is AA's international monthly journal, published continuously since its first issue in June 1944. The AA pamphlet on AA Grapevine describes its scope and purpose this way: "As an integral part of Alcoholics Anonymous since 1944, the Grapevine publishes articles that reflect the full diversity of experience and thought found within the A.A. Fellowship, as does La Viña, the bimonthly Spanish-language magazine, first published in 1996. No one viewpoint or philosophy dominates their pages, and in determining content, the editorial staff relies on the principles of the Twelve Traditions."

In addition to magazines, AA Grapevine, Inc. also produces an app, books, eBooks, audiobooks and other items. It also offers a Grapevine Online subscription, which includes: new stories weekly, AudioGrapevine (the audio version of the magazine), the Grapevine Story Archive and the current issue of Grapevine and La Viña in HTML format. For more information on AA Grapevine, or to subscribe to any of these, please visit the magazine's website at www.aagrapevine.org or write to:

AA Grapevine, Inc., 475 Riverside Drive, New York, NY 10115